Openly Aging

*The 4 Pillars of How to Keep
Control of Your Aging Journey*

Allison O'Shea

This book is not intended for use as a source of legal, health,
medical, or financial advice. All readers are advised to seek the
services of competent professionals in these fields.

Disclaimer:
Everyone's situation is one-hundred-percent unique. Aging is a
universal issue, but as you work through this book you will realize
that your aging journey will not look like anyone else's and vice
versa.

The advice and strategies found within may not be suitable for
every situation. This work is sold with the understanding that
neither the author nor the publisher is held responsible for the
results accrued from the advice in this book.

For more information, visit https://openlyaging.com.

ISBN 978-1-961757-44-8 (paperback)
ISBN 978-1-961757-45-5 (eBook)
LCCN: 2024904545

Publisher: Hybrid Global Publishing, New York, NY
Cover Design by Kelly Nielsen, Studio 92
https://www.studio92.us/

Dedication

This book is dedicated to my parents who have always been there for me and always encouraged me to dream big and go after what I desire!

Also, my wonderful husband, Chris, and our two children, Jack and Emily. You inspire me every day to be the best version of myself.

TABLE OF CONTENTS

INTRODUCTION

Why do we hate to acknowledge that we are aging? Why are so many of us resentful and angry about aging and how we are aging? For twenty years I have worked directly with aging individuals and their families, and it gave me a perspective on aging that I hope will help others be a little more proactive and less reactive to their aging journey. You can put a plan in place for your aging journey which will help you stay independent longer and on your terms. The catch is you must be a little self-aware and willing to talk about the elephant in the room...AGING.

The other elephant in the room is that everyone who starts to read this book will not finish it. Of course, I hope that my compelling writing will keep you fully engaged until the end, but do not worry if you are the type of person who wants to move to straight into working on the pillars. For more resources, including scheduling a private consultation with me, go to: www.openlyaging.com/book.

* * *

The year is 1994 and I am spending my twelfth summer of life babysitting a three-month-old baby in my neighborhood for eight hours at a time...crazy! I currently have a twelve-year-old, so it amazes me that someone would trust a twelve-year-old to watch not just their kid but a very helpless three-month-old. There was no denying that I was mature for twelve, but in all honesty, caregiving came and comes very naturally to me. I find it interesting to look back at my formative years and look at them through a new lens as an adult.

I have realized that my parents were also caregivers. We moved from Georgia to Ohio when I was twelve to be there to help my grandfather when my grandmother got sick. She passed two years later, and we were there to support and care for my grandfather who had had a tough time losing his beloved wife. We also had a neighbor who came on challenging times with their family, and low and behold, Mrs. D became part of our lives. She was at every holiday and even gave us a puppy for Christmas one year without asking my parents. These are just two examples, but my mom was simply a magnet for aging neighbors who needed a little family, and she would bring them into ours. Going back to my babysitting enterprise…by the time I was fourteen I had a client list of over thirty families. I was busy and had more extra money than all my friends, but I also discovered the freedom of working and have had some sort of employment since the age of twelve. The end of my eighth-grade year I told my dad that I wanted to work with children with disabilities and, at the time, felt this was the career path I wanted to explore.

You may ask why, at fourteen, was I already thinking about my future career? My dad had a motto that he told his kids often, "Find what you love to do and the money will come"; basically, to be thoughtful about what I would want my future career to be and then in order to truly be happy and successful at it, it needed to include the skills I naturally possess. Therefore, no one was surprised when I wanted to explore options that involved caregiving. So, once I told my dad that I was interested in helping those with disabilities he jumped right in to connect me with opportunities that would build on those interests and skills.

This was the year that I was introduced to a wonderful place called Recreation Unlimited. My parents hosted a large holiday party each year and since I told my dad that I wanted to work with kids with disabilities, he took the opportunity that night to introduce me to Paul. Paul was Executive Director of Recreation Unlimited. RU was a summer camp for kids and adults with disabilities located in Ashley, Ohio. At fourteen years old I spent the first of five consecutive summers at RU.

My role was to be a counselor. The camp assigned me two campers each week who I would support during the camp. This was an overnight camp, so I was responsible for all my campers 24/7. The camp was split up into separate groups each week. One week would be adults with developmental disabilities and then there would be a kids' DD week. There would be a week for adults with physical disabilities and one for kids. The RU camp was a place for these adults and kids to go where they could be their authentic selves and do "camp" activities that were one hundred percent adapted to their needs. RU was a haven, not only for the campers but for myself, and I think for most of the counselors who worked there. I learned a lot about caregiving especially when I look back and think of all the personal care duties I was performing when I was between the ages of fourteen and eighteen.

One week I was taking care of a young lady named Amanda who had Spina bifida and the next week I was supporting Alex, a ten-year-old who had a severe seizure disorder, and thus, required me to place a magnet on his head about every fifteen minutes when he started to seize. It was during this very formative and life-changing experience when I was introduced to the profession of a Certified Therapeutic Recreation Specialist® (CTRS), which is the qualified professional providing recreational therapy services. Many of the college-age counselors were in school working toward this degree. It was then that I decided that was the route I wanted to go.

As you can imagine Therapeutic Recreation is not a common major, so my list of potential colleges was small. I landed in Belmont, North Carolina at Belmont Abbey College. I professed to anyone who would listen that I wanted to work with kids. I soon found out that finding a role as a Recreational Therapist working with kids was challenging. I struggled with finding a job and spent the year after I graduated serving drinks at a sports bar in uptown Charlotte. Eventually, I had to become creative and figure out what I was qualified to do and start making moves toward my dream career.

It was at this time that I started interviewing for Activity Assistant roles in senior living. Looking back, I had no idea where I was applying and the level of care I would be expected to provide. I did not know the difference between skilled nursing, assisted living, and memory care. Like most of you reading this book I had no idea the different options available and how they worked.

Finally, I was offered a position as an Activity Assistant at a community called Oakdale Heights in Charlotte, NC. Since 2005 it has not only changed names but companies many times. My role was to create and facilitate all the programming in the Memory Care neighborhood. My first day I spent walking around getting to know the residents and introducing myself to the associates. I grabbed a beach ball and went into one of the family rooms and started throwing a ball to each resident and asking them questions. I was immediately told by the associates that "they can't talk." I said, "Thank you," and completely ignored their comment. I discovered that not only did the residents engage with me, but they thoroughly enjoyed the banter *and* they smiled. That moment sticks out to me because not only did I recognize my confidence in ignoring negative feedback, but I also got so much personal joy in creating moments of fun for the residents.

I knew I was right where I suppose to be and was truly fascinated by the Dementia process and how it affected each person so differently. It was during this first year of my career that I became aware of the aging industry. There was a service for everything, and it was growing fast as more people were aging. I dove headfirst into my career and within three years I was the Executive Director of a small memory care community. During those three years I married my college sweetheart and we moved to Durham, North Carolina.

For the next eighteen years I grew as an Executive Director. My buildings got bigger and bigger, and I was able to be selective in what companies I would work for as I was recruited often and had a good reputation. My last experience in senior living was that I was able to open a senior living community, which means create the policies, hire the associates, and create a training program. I was able to create the culture I wanted and ensure that the building, from the beginning, exemplified the culture. It was a tremendous change from the many times in my career that I was hired to go into a troubled community and fix the issues and bring the correct culture. I was doing okay directing a building that had two-hundred residents and about one-hundred-and-fifty associates and then…COVID-19. I am sure I do not need a lot of details about why COVID-19 was incredibly challenging as the Executive Director of senior living. Families could not see their loved ones; associates were having to balance having their children at home and coming into work. We were all scared of this unknown virus, and the fear could be paralyzing, so as the leader of all these people I had to keep control and confidence in the decisions I needed to make. I spent a lot of time away from my family and the ninety days we thought it was going to take to go back to normal turned into two years.

Like most people I started to realize that my time in senior living had run its course. Not only did I need more flexibility for my family, but my heart was just not in it anymore. I needed a new challenge and adventure, but what should I do? Like many people contemplating a life change, I sat and wrote a list of all the tasks and responsibilities I loved to do in my role and the areas in which I was bored or burned out. The list helped me see that I genuinely loved and felt strongly about my ability to educate people going through the aging journey. I had found throughout my career that most people have no idea what resources are out there and how to use them. They would move into senior living because they did not have a lot of options, but they still did not understand how it worked and what to expect. I also loved helping families have honest conversations. I realized I have talent in feeling comfortable bringing up tough conversations but doing it in a way where no one is offended while progress is made in getting everyone on the same page. I wanted to use these skills, experiences, and desire to help.

In January of 2022 I founded *Openly Aging,* and I am an Aging Advisor. I support individuals in looking at their situation and creating aging plans that make sense and help them maintain their independence.

1

ADDRESSING THE ELEPHANT
IN THE ROOM

After twenty years of working directly with aging individuals and their family units I have a unique perspective on aging. I was able to witness thousands of individuals age, and even though aging is a universal issue, everyone's personal aging journey is one-hundred-percent unique to them. Through my experience I saw individuals who aged well and embraced the moment in life they were in, but I also witnessed people aging full of resentment and anger. They felt out of control and felt that others were making decisions for them.

Most of the time they were not wrong, but someone was helping them with decisions because they had never talked about their goals and had not put any plans in place to support their goals. They were also probably resistant and in denial of anything anyone told them about their abilities. On the other side of this I witnessed family support systems overwhelmed, resentful, and frustrated. They wanted the best for their loved one, but due to lack of planning, communication, and denial, a crisis occurred and now a family member had to put their whole life on hold to get their loved one safe and settled, *and* they had to do this while working and taking care of their family. The cherry on top was that the person they were supporting was angry and making things exceedingly difficult. This combination does not make for a happy family unit.

As I continued to see the above scenario happen repeatedly, I realized there is a missing role in the aging industry. We are so used to being reactive to aging that the idea of being proactive is not one people embrace easily. My goal with *Openly Aging* is to educate and advise aging individuals and help them put a comprehensive aging plan in place. There are multiple components to aging that are unpredictable, but my experience has shown me that as you work through and plan within the four pillars that I am going to detail in the following chapters, you can be more in control.

The "Why"

I hope to provide to you, the reader, the "why" of the importance of taking a proactive approach to your aging plans. My extensive experience has given me a unique perspective that will be invaluable to your journey. We need to learn to embrace our aging and be self-aware enough to be thoughtful on decisions that make the most sense for us to stay independent longer. We must be able to say, "This is the last chapter of my life and I want to live it while being in control." We should be grateful for the experiences we have had but also be content with where we are now. We need to move past our regrets and things that did not go how we would have hoped.

To find peace and joy we need to embrace where we are today and prepare for what may come tomorrow. The process of planning for your aging journey can be emotional but it will be worth it, and it will be a gift to your support system as they will be able to enjoy time with you and not feel overwhelmed or lost on how to help.

Let Us Uplevel Your Aging Journey!

2

WHAT YOU NEED TO
KNOW ABOUT AGING

I am going to start this journey with you with some statistics that I feel will help us understand why we need to be more proactive with our aging plan. Bear with me if you are not a data-driven person like me.

According to The National Council on Aging, in 2023 there are fifty-six million Americans sixty-five years and up. It is projected that by 2060 ninety-five million Americans will be in the sixty-five plus age category.

And my favorite statistic: The Institute on Aging says that in 1900 there were only one-hundred-thousand Americans who were eighty-five or older. This statistic really struck me, especially considering that in 2010 there were 5.5 million Americans eighty-five or older. The projection is that there will be nineteen million Americans eighty-five or older by 2050. The eighty-five plus category is the fastest growing age group within the sixty-five and up group. Or as my dad says, "Sixty-five and death." Sorry, a little humor.

Why these statistics are important as we work to have more control of our aging journey is because according to the National Institute of Health, almost sixty percent of individuals eighty-five years and older need some sort of support from a family caregiver due to "health problems and functional limitations." If you have been lucky enough to see your parents or grandparents age, think about when they were in the eighty-to-ninety-five range. What support did they need? I also want to be clear that this statistic is not necessarily referring to support for Activities of Daily Living or what we call ADLs. Showering, grooming, and toileting are examples of ADLs. This refers to emergency support, ensuring medications are picked up, food is in the house, support during medical appointments, and transportation, if needed, just to name a few.

So now you know that the likelihood of living to be at least eighty-five years old is higher than it has ever been in American history and that sixty percent of people will need some sort of support from another person when they are eighty-five or older. Doesn't this make you want to plan for that time in your life? You may be one of the lucky ones and continue to be one-hundred-percent independent at eighty-five, but guess what? This is a predictor that you will live to see your nineties. Research shows that seventy-five percent of individuals ninety and older need support from another person.

Introduction to the 4-Pillar Aging Plan

While we work through the four pillars of aging success, please realize that we are planning and preparing for this phase of our life. If you prepare for the time when you need a little more support, it will ensure that you will be prepared if your health declines sooner than your eighty-fifth year. My Four-Pillar Aging Plan is an insurance policy that will be there to guide and support while you work through your own personal aging journey. I also hope that by preparing and working through the principles that you will enter this phase of life less fearful and increase your morale to a place where you can appreciate where you are and all you have built.

I should also add that for the first ten or so years of my eighteen years working in senior living I honestly thought crisis was normal. I have since changed my core values surrounding this and feel that if more of the individuals, I saw in crisis had thought about the four pillars I have identified then the crisis they were dealing with would have been less traumatic and more organized.

* * *

To change gears just for a minute, I feel it is important to note that if we are going to discuss aging and how to keep control and maintain our independence longer, we need to first define Ageism.

Ageism is "prejudice or discrimination based on the person's age."

We also need to have a constructive conversation about ageism and how it plays a role in how we plan or should I say NOT plan for our aging journey. It is no surprise when I write "our society prioritizes youth." We look at youth as a goal, which is completely ludicrous. We cannot *achieve* youth. We are either young or old, but no matter which age bracket you fall into right at this moment, the bottom line is that WE ARE ALL CURRENTLY AGING. I am not as young as I was when

I started writing this chapter and I will be older by the time this book comes out. That is a fact! Youth cannot be a goal—it is a subjective concept. What this idea of acquiring youth has left us with is the idea that aging is shameful and, therefore, we do not discuss it, thus allowing for the concept of Ageism to thrive.

Ageism occurs because as we age, others tend to view us as dependent, weaker, in denial, and resistant to talking about our aging issues. Until we can open the dialogue about our aging journeys and plan for what may come, others will view us as dependent, weaker, in denial, and resistant to support. As aging individuals, it is our responsibility to take back control of our aging journeys and that will help combat the ageism we find today in our society.

What I found interesting when researching for this book was that all the websites and articles on how to teach people to *not* have ageist thoughts or actions were directed at "younger" individuals and how they can be less ageist and more accepting of aging individuals in their life. This made me step back and evaluate my relationship with aging and how I could be presenting ageist behaviors. Then I realized we will never get rid of ageism if we do not directly talk to "aging individuals."

Why are we ageist as a society?

Why do we view aging individuals as "less than?"

Then it struck me! Due to our obsession with youth, we have enabled the aging members of our community to lack the ability, knowledge, and overall expectation to talk or communicate about aging concerns. In my work as an Aging Advisor with individuals who value having a plan in place and want the education to age more independently, they often say that when they mention their aging with their family they are met with, "We don't want to talk about this."

We cannot stop ageism until we get our aging friends, family, and neighbors to feel comfortable talking about their aging journey and their goals and desires. This will not happen if their family cannot or will not deal with the fact that their loved one is getting older. Do not let your family's uncomfortableness with aging stop you from planning for your journey. You have all the control, and this book will help you wield it in the right way.

3

WHY DO I NEED A PLAN, ANYWAYS?

I have seen many unique situations, but the two true stories in this chapter are an example of why preparing for your aging journey is the healthiest thing you can do for not only yourself but the ones you love.

Scott & His Mother Jane

I met Scott while I was the Executive Director of a community that had three levels of care: 1) independent living, 2) assisted living, and 3) memory care. Scott's mother Jane lived two hours away in the house and town where she had lived for fifty years. Jane's son was going back and forth a few times a week because Jane needed support with appointments and meals. Scott had talked to his mom for years about moving closer to him and his family. Jane refused and genuinely thought she was successfully living in her home without any local support. Scott felt a sense of guilt for wanting to take his mom from what she had known for fifty years just to make his life easier, and that made conversations around moving difficult. He finally realized that his immediate family was suffering because of the time he spent away from them to make sure his mom was okay. The realization brought him into my community to learn a little more about what his mom's options were, and then, of course, getting advice on how to approach his mom. Scott's mom, Jane, continued to be resistant to moving until she encountered a medical crisis which resulted in her lying on the floor in her home for over twelve hours with a broken hip.

The situation left Scott no choice but to move his mom closer to him as she needed more physical support. In an instant, Jane lost all her control in choosing her living situation. The loss of control, even if it was in her best interest, left her angry and resentful. The situation also left her with her only option being assisted living as she had missed the opportunity to move into an independent apartment, patio home, or condominium. Her morale was extremely low, and she was never able to accept her situation. She spent the last few years of her life angry, resentful, and sad. Not only did her response to losing control leave Scott with constant feelings of guilt but it also affected his time with his mom and their relationship suffered because it was difficult for him to see her so angry at him.

Sheila

Now let us talk about Sheila. Sheila came to one of my communities on her own and with her own agenda. Sheila lived in another state but was visiting her daughter and her family for the holidays. The previous year she was starting to realize that her medical appointments were becoming overwhelming and she was not able to travel as easily. In her heart Sheila knew living closer to her daughter was the right decision to not only protect her independence but to ensure her daughter was able to provide the support she may need one day.

From Sheila's first visit to the community, it took a year for her to move. But what she did was take that year and tour communities, educate herself on what resources she might need as she aged, and talk with her family on what would be the best for them. She moved into Independent Living, one-hundred-percent independent, where she could meet new friends, enjoy quality time with grandkids, and be in complete control of her aging. She was happy, engaged, and healthy. She made a big life decision at the right time and for the right reasons; therefore, she will be independent longer as all her needs are being met and her relationship with her family is strong and healthy.

As a disclosure, most of my experience is based in senior living so my stories do represent a lot of senior living, but I do believe that senior living is only one option of many. More on that as we move through the pillars. I do not want to scare you off with the thought that I am going to try to convince you that senior living is your only option.

* * *

My question to you: Do you want to be angry, in denial, and resentful like Jane? Or do you want to be in control, happy, and mentally and emotionally healthy like Sheila? In the twenty years I have worked with aging individuals I have seen the two scenarios above play out many times. I want to choose to be in control and I know you do, too, especially if you are reading this book.

So how do we keep control of our aging journey?

It starts with our mindset. No one wants to think about getting older, and sometimes the choices we must make are ones we never thought we would be choosing. During my time in senior living when I would coach my sales team, I would remind them that no one is touring senior living because they are bored. Something is going on that has made them realize that they need to start gathering more information on options.

Even residents who came to us fully independent had some realization that brought them in to tour—perhaps a medical diagnosis, loneliness, fear of the future, or the desire to be closer to their adult children. Regardless of the reason, it was our job to show them the quality of life they would have by making such a big decision, a decision none of us thought we would be making. For us to be prepared to make these big decisions with clear minds and hearts, there are a few mindset changes we need to make.

We must start talking and acknowledging the elephant in the room. We need to get out of denial and become self-aware of who we are, our goals and desires, and the challenges we face, emotionally and physically. Having an understanding and appreciation for who we are and where our life decisions have taken us is not only empowering, but it will also help our plan be clear and concise. Each of the four pillars I will discuss in this book will help you learn a little bit more about yourself and how the next step in life will be based on the decisions you have made thus far.

We must not let fear paralyze us but use our abilities to feel empowered. While we are independent and healthy, we need to start asking questions. I read somewhere that the three reasons we do not talk about aging is because we are fearful of *dependency, disease, and death*. Shouldn't these three likely inevitable scenarios be the reason we do plan for our aging journey?

Support services as you age are not cheap. There are many options for services and using them correctly will save you both time and money.

We need to focus on becoming an educated consumer and not a vulnerable consumer.

Let us try to reduce the likelihood of people taking advantage of us by educating ourselves. We need to use our time when we are independent and healthy to become educated consumers. As I said, aging needs are expensive and we need to make sure we understand just how much things cost, how business models work, what we should be doing today to prepare for tomorrow, and what makes the most sense for our personal situation. In other words, let us get our heads out of the sand.

Our society is very reactive. A perfect example is how we prescribe medicine. If we have an issue, our doctor prescribes medication and any side effects of those medications we treat with more medications. We have this same approach with aging. We do not do any planning for our aging years until something happens, then we must make expensive and big decisions while feeling scared and overwhelmed. Or, in all honesty, this is the moment where your family steps in and starts making decisions for you.

Why can't we be proactive and figure out goals and desires before a crisis occurs? Or even better, make transitions before we need support? Making decisions early will also keep us independent longer because we will be in the right environment with our support system close by or we will have a professional support system identified and rapport built. So, if we decline or have issues, we have a checks and balances system already set up to bring in services sooner rather than later to help slow the decline.

Now that we can move past denial and into self-awareness, use our fear of aging to feel empowered, get ourselves educated on potential resources and start being proactive and not reactive, we are ready to uplevel our aging journey and put a plan in place to keep control.

There are no right or wrong answers. Just like aging is a fact, so is your current situation and how it affects your aging journey. Each answer has more questions to follow but there is no right or wrong decisions or answers.

Your plan should fit your finances and not the other way around. I have found many people do not talk about aging because they are so fearful of money and that they will not have enough. That is a perfect reason creating an aging plan that fits your finances is crucial. If you have money regrets, you need to move on and just be honest about your situation. Making decisions sooner than later will allow you to be independent longer and, therefore, save you money. You will be a believer by the end of this book!

This process is going to be emotional. Anytime you must come to terms with life decisions, the good and the bad, it can bring up emotions of regret, fear, and sadness. We cannot stop our planning because we are emotional. Look at this work as therapy so you can live this part of your life with contentment. Embracing this work is a choice we each must make. Thinking of aging, and dare I say planning, for the last chapter of our life can be hard, but to live it full of joy, gratitude, and peace we must acknowledge what brought us here and how to best move forward.

I developed the four pillars of aging success because I saw they were the four most common themes that individuals dealt with when they encountered a crisis. It is without fail that when you think of an aging crisis you have witnessed or dealt with, it fits into one of the pillars we are going to discuss. Now let us dive into the four pillars.

4

PILLAR 1: SUPPORT SYSTEM

If you are lucky enough to have seen your parents age, what was your involvement in their aging journey? Were you the local family with the primary caregiver role (whether minor or intense) or did you witness it from afar? Part of the journey you will go on in this book is coming to terms with how you view aging. The experiences you have had witnessing or supporting someone who is aging directly affects how you view your aging journey and how proactive or reactive you are.

I have found that we think we are never going to age or need the support we witness older loved ones needing. It is a true phenomenon to me...I guess to protect our psyche we legitimately pretend that our aging journey will be free of issues, and we will just fall asleep and never wake up again, never needing to leave our home or pay for additional support. I wish this scenario for everyone and that we would never have to activate our plan, but it comes with low odds. My husband's Aunt Elsie was one of those people who just passed in her sleep after drinking her two vodka clubs and playing a few hands of poker with friends. She died peacefully in an assisted living situation that took many months and a few health crises to convince her to live there.

If you have read this far, you read the statistic that many of us will live to be eighty-five years or older and sixty percent of us will need support from someone due to medical or functional limitations.

In your life experience, have you been a support system to someone; perhaps parents, aunts, uncles, or maybe a neighbor or close friend?

If you were eighty-five today, who in your life would you consider your support system?

Primary Support System

First, let us define a primary support system. A primary support system could be private such as an adult child or other close relative/friend, or it could be a professional such as a Care Manager. Your primary support system *cannot* be anyone who is in the same age category as you. Your primary support system needs to be someone younger who has agreed to be there to support you. In this chapter we will work through how to identify that support system and why it is important for all the steps that follow.

In my extensive experience, the statistic I mentioned previously (*many of us will live to be eighty-five years or older and sixty percent of us will need support from someone due to medical of functional limitations*) is right on target if not a little low, in my opinion. Even my residents who were one-hundred-percent independent did need support in areas they never needed support in before. An example of this would be getting medicine when they were sick. As we age, a common cold hits us a little differently and can create a situation where we may not be steady on our feet, we may get dehydrated very easily, and driving to a store or the doctor's office or urgent care can be challenging and may not, frankly, be realistic.

By being proactive, thoughtful, and identifying your support system ahead of time, you would be able to rest and stay safe in your home while your support system is able to bring medicine and whatever else you may need. This will ensure that no more damage occurs like a fall or a virus getting worse because of trying to do too much, and it will keep you independent longer. I know this example seems simple, but I cannot tell you how often little situations like this arose for people over the age of eighty-five.

I have also witnessed many examples of people who did not have a support system and refused to acknowledge their decline. A person would get into a car and try to get medicine or take expired medicine at home because they were unable to leave. No one checks in on them and they get dehydrated and end up falling and going to the hospital which leads to rehab and potentially losing all ability to live alone. All control gone and it all started with a simple cold.

Joan

Let us talk about Joan and why identifying your support system when you are independent is crucial in working through your aging plan. Joan is the mother of five kids. Three are local to her and two live in different states. Joan is aging and has done well in the house she lives in, but she is starting to have more doctor's appointments and, unfortunately, driving is becoming an issue. She can drive, but she is starting to not feel comfortable going to unfamiliar places or driving when the sun is setting. Of her three kids who live locally, two visit her once a week, and one, her daughter Leah, checks in on her daily. Leah is a professional with high-school-aged children...in other words, she is busy. For Joan to get to her doctor's appointments, church, or other activities with friends she relies on Leah to help get her there. In all honesty Joan's needs have slowly increased to the point where Leah must be involved daily.

This is normally how it happens. Leah is starting to feel overwhelmed with the extra demand on her time and also trying to balance being available for her husband and children. She would love for her mom to consider a different living situation but is scared to bring it up. Her local siblings do not agree that a different living situation is necessary. Joan is not against moving because she is starting to feel lonely and she feels a lot of guilt about how much time Leah is taking to support her, but she also does not know how to make the transition.

Does she have enough money?

Where would she go?

How do you even start to move out of your house of over thirty years?

All that Joan needs is for someone to walk her through the process, and she will be fine; she is not resistant and knows it might be time. Her local children who see her once a week always talk to her about staying in her home and she, of course, trusts what they say, yet she also knows that Leah is struggling. Leah does not want to rock the boat and not have support from her siblings and Joan does not want to upset anyone, so they continue this course where Joan is not getting everything she could be receiving socially and medically. No changes are made, so both Joan and Leah will not have the quality of life they both deserve.

This scenario is quite common but does not have to happen if you identify your support system and inform all others in your life who that support person is. If Joan had told her other children that Leah was going to be the primary support system, Leah would have the confidence to make the decisions she may need to make. Joan would know she had chosen someone she could trust and feel comfortable with to oversee her aging goals and desires.

It is these situations that occur over and over that increase your chances of losing control. Putting simple solutions in place today can help you avoid having to move to a higher level of care.

Remember in my disclaimer… "we are all aging, but our aging experiences are one-hundred-percent unique." Aging allies or people serving as support systems should be aware that their personal goals and desires as they age might be vastly different than the person they are supporting. Identifying who you want as your support system will be the way you can make sure your plans are followed. It is so common for aging parents to assign the role of Power of Attorney to their oldest child. If this person is the one you can trust the most and you feel that they listen and will not put their own expectations on you, that is great. If you sit back and realize that your middle child or your niece is the person you trust the most and who you feel will listen to you effectively, then it is okay to choose them as your Power of Attorney and support system. Sometimes for us to pick the right support system we need to sit and have discussions with those involved. Later in this chapter I will present ten things to ask and think about when choosing your support system.

Think about the people in your life; perhaps you have adult children. How many children do you have? Of your children, can you identify one you feel would be the best to support you? This will be one of those times throughout this journey where you will need to put emotions aside, not worry about offending other children or family, and think practically and factually about what your options are for a support system and why one person would be better than another. There is also an option for identifying more than one person, but as we move through the process you will see that each person should have their own role and specific "jobs." Let us get on with it.

Here are the ten things to think about when identifying your support system. By thinking through the items below, you will protect yourself and your support system from being unsuccessful.

Consider the following when it comes to support systems:

1. Your support person needs to be someone you trust with your physical self but also your money. Ideally this is one person; however, if necessary, it can be two people, one who helps you make decisions for your physical well-being and one who handles your money. If you have two people, then you will need to be mindful and strategic about how to communicate with both parties and how they communicate with each other.

2. Does this person share the same core values as you regarding aging?

3. You have evaluated their lifestyle and how they manage time and attention, and you are confident they can manage additional responsibilities. You need to look at how many children they have, career growth and aspirations, and time management skills.
4. You feel this person is strong in holding your goals and desires as a priority over other's opinions so there is no risk for exploitation.
5. Where does this person live? They do not have to be local, but it is an important consideration as we move through the pillars. You may need to have a secondary support system...more to come on that.
6. How is their health and lifestyle? This is not a deal breaker, but if they are not in the best health for their age, then you need to identify a secondary support person who is part of the journey from the beginning.
7. Are they financially stable? Are you still supporting them? If you have concerns about money management, you need to talk with an estate planner to ensure you secure your funds appropriately, so you have enough to take care of your aging journey.
8. How do they handle their personal relationships?
9. Are you able to have open and honest conversations with them? Do they possess emotional intelligence?
10. If they have concerns, are you able to listen to them and not get defensive?

After you assess your relationships and those who may be able to be your support system, if you still feel that you can't identify someone, you need to be educated on a professional support system. There are a host of wonderful professionals out there whose entire career is focused on supporting aging individuals.

> ➢ Geriatric Care Managers
> ➢ Patient Advocates
> ➢ Life Care Managers

Use these titles and words when looking for a professional support system.

Unfortunately, in our reactive world, the first time most individuals find out about the professions above is when they have a crisis that resulted in having to bring this professional on to leave the hospital or function at all. Bringing in these professionals at a time when you cannot interview, understand, or when you do not have a choice is the worst time because you will spend more money and pay them to do crisis management. If you identified that a professional support system makes the most sense for your aging journey, then you should know this long before a crisis or decline happens. This circles back to being self-aware and facing the facts of your life. There is nothing wrong with needing a professional support system and, if nothing else, you are smart for being able to acknowledge it. Here is the secret: Most people are introduced to a professional support system *after* a crisis has occurred, and this feels backwards to me.

If you are going to need a professional support system you should plan for it ahead of time by vetting, interviewing, and hiring *before* you technically need their service. The goal is that you have prepared and planned for an independent aging journey so you will never need them to come in and help make decisions for you. If they do have to enter that role, wouldn't you want an established relationship with them where you have told them your goals, desires, and plans? The clients I support and work with know that I will first help them identify a professional support system as part of their plan. I advise them to vet, interview, and hire sooner rather than later.

Meeting with your professional support system every six months to have coffee, lay out your plan, and talk through issues that arise with your plan is smart. By doing this you have ensured not only that you have someone looking out for you on your terms, which will keep you independent longer and save you money, but you can be assured that you have an advocate and ally when things get tough and out of your control.

This profession attracts master's level social workers, so you need to budget and be knowledgeable on the best way to use them based on your unique situation. You need to know how to vet and interview for this position. The price as of today is $125-$175 an hour on average. Securing your support person early will keep you independent longer so maybe you would spend $175 every six months and increase slowly. Their entire role consists of noticing any declines and talking to you about all your aging concerns. This is an insurance plan to help you save money longer and stay healthier longer.

A **professional support system** can also be used as a primary or secondary contact. If a person's primary support system is not local, having a professional support system is necessary for my clients. Review the ten questions I posed earlier in this chapter to ask potential support persons. If you have concerns about any of the ten points, having a professional support system in your back pocket is an excellent idea, as calling them in the middle of a crisis will not benefit you. Having an established relationship beforehand is the ideal situation so they can get to know your primary support system and you can work out a communication system that works for everyone.

Here is the deal: a care manager, patient advocate, or life care manager is not the only option if you cannot identify a personal primary support system. If you have money concerns, you need to see a lawyer immediately so you can learn about state assistance and your state's minimum income for assistance. You will need to understand the assistance programs you are eligible for and how best to work with them. Bringing in support or moving to a supportive environment earlier than later is how you stay independent longer.

Another thing to note about identifying support systems is that you have a few options if they live in different states. You need to educate yourself on those states and the associated financial benefits, taxes, and other options available. You may find that one state has better options for you and that is the support system you choose.

Once you have identified your person or persons, you need to ask these two crucial questions:

1. **Do all your legal documents reflect the support system you identified?** I recommend that if you are over the age of sixty-five and have not gotten your legal aging documents reviewed in the last five years, it is an excellent idea to do it. Also, if you have moved to another state and have not had your documents reviewed, this is another reason to visit an Estate Planning Attorney.

2. **Have you communicated and asked the person(s) you identified as your support system if they are okay with the role?** Your support system needs to be given the opportunity to express any concerns

they may have with fulfilling the role and they must be told that you are working through the pillars so you will be able to present them with an organized, well thought out, strategic aging plan that will make their support system role easier.

As a final note, if you do not identify a support system and do not get your documents in order to support your decision and something traumatic and/or unexpected happens, it leaves the door open for someone you don't want in charge of your decisions to sneak their way in, including an unwanted family member or a guardian of the state.

Do you want the last chapter of your life to be determined by a stranger or someone who you do not trust?

If you need further guidance please go to www. openlyaging.com/book *where you will find resources to start creating your Aging Plan.*

5

PILLAR 2: "HOME"

The number one comment I hear when helping my clients is that they have a goal of aging at home. Most of the time it is the home that they have lived in for twenty to sixty years. Remember, I said "there is no right or wrong answer" so staying in your home is your right, but you must PLAN for it. You need to plan for it at least seven years before you may need to make decisions.

But…is staying in that home the best choice for you and your aging journey? Will you be isolated, which would lead to a miserable last few years? Do you have a personal or paid support system that is willing to be the manager of your life? How much does it cost to maintain the home? I know I sound critical about staying in your home and most of the stories I share do involve a different living environment, but if you bought a home without thinking of aging in it, most likely it's not going to be the best living situation long-term if you desire sustained independence and control the longest.

There are a few aging individuals I have met over the years who, after assessing their situation, determined that it was best for them to stay in their home, but to be honest, that is most likely the case because they do not have ANY other option due to lack of funds. They make the most of their situation, but my goal is to help people live their *best* life and be in the place they WANT to be and not the ONLY place they *can* be. Financially I believe it makes the most sense to initiate a transition at a specific moment identified by you and your Aging Advisor, but I also believe that transitions at certain points in our life are good for our cognition. Our brains need to develop new connections at certain intervals in our life.

Think about downsizing to a condominium or patio home in an area that caters to aging individuals who are like-minded. Consider all the new people you would meet yet still maintain your privacy, all the new roads you would have to learn, the new stores you would discover. Everything would be NEW, and our brain likes new. Doing crosswords or Sudoku every day only works one part of the brain; do things to work the other areas. Change directions sporadically, that is my biggest advice!

I would like to add that there is something to be said about intergenerational living, but this also needs to be an intentional decision where the younger residents also have a goal of supporting their aging neighbors. Again, I repeat, if you believe staying in your home is your best option knowing all the risks, I salute you. Where you age is one hundred percent your decision if you are educated and making decisions with a clear mind—you can put a plan in place to make it happen so everyone is supported and you have given consideration to your finances to support it. You have also put triggers in place for the next transition if necessary...but remember the support system that you chose; if they start making comments and having *conversations*, you need to listen to them. You cannot go into this decision delusional and uneducated.

For those who are ready to start talking about their next adventures let us get down to it. I must be honest: While drafting this book I have had moments where I got stuck because this topic is so big. Just remember, "Aging is Universal, but your situation is one-hundred-percent Unique." Breaking all this down is so hard because it becomes a rabbit hole of many options and paths.

I am going to be very high level here:

When I work with clients, we work in a flow chart as shown below.

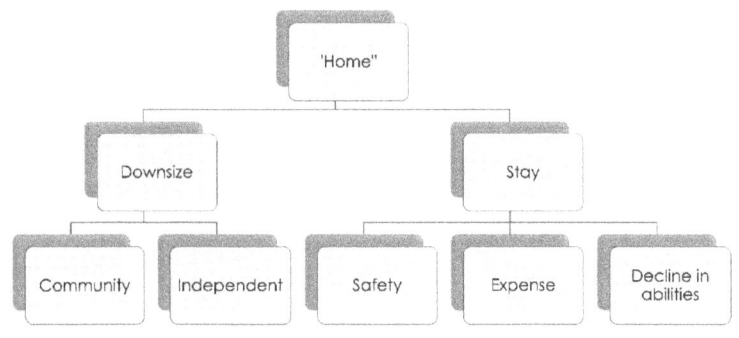

When you know you are going to downsize, not today but in a few years, you must decide what exactly that is going to look like. You truly have two options:

1) A Private Residence in a Private Community.

This would be a patio home or condominium. What this option does not have is the social component built in. There is nothing wrong with it, but it means that you need to be very intentional regarding your social engagement and create a plan for it. This is the fourth pillar, and I will discuss it more in Chapter 7. An Aging Advisor can walk you through this and you can go to www.openlyaging.com/book. Most of my clients start with this living situation, building in triggers that aid them in knowing when the next transition might be in their best interest. The important thing about an Aging Plan is that because you have thought it through, you will have already chosen the next transitions for when or if that trigger occurs.

2) Community Living

If you have identified that a built-in social engagement situation works better for you and your personality, a community living situation might be the best option for you. One of the biggest myths I come across is that the only living options as we age are moving from home to independent living or assisted living. There are so many other options! I want this to be one of the biggest lessons that you take from this book. **You need to arm yourself with education and explore.** Here is a list of options to give you keywords to search:

- o Co-housing
- o Active Aging Community
- o 55+
- o CCRC – Continuing Care Retirement Community
- o Independent Living
- o Assisted Living
- o Memory Care
- o Skilled Nursing

As an Aging Advisor I educate my clients on all living options that are available to them, and we work through questions to help them determine which type or types of living environments would be best for them. I cannot stress enough that educating yourself on all available options keeps *you* in the driver's seat of control.

These are examples of some of the questions that help us determine what type of living situation will make the most sense:

- Where does your identified support system reside?
- Are there medical diagnosis/history that could predict needing care as you age?
- What do your finances look like?
- How do you socialize?

Now, pause for a moment and take a breath because it is important to understand that a transition to a new living environment is not something you are doing tomorrow. I do believe we should transition to an appropriate housing option *before* we think we NEED to; however, what you are doing while working through this pillar is eliminating living situations that do not apply to you while getting a full education on the ones that do. Education allows you to understand the pros and cons of each option. It also enables you to put triggers in place to help you determine when a transition needs to occur. I will go into triggers in depth in the next chapter but think of it as a black-and-white occurrence (amount of money being spent, diagnosis or decline) that helps you take out the emotion of decision-making so you can plan based on facts.

For many of my clients, we work through this pillar in two stages, exemplified in the story below.

Julie lives in a ranch-style house and is very socially active at church and in the neighborhood. She wants to stay home as long as she can. What does *as long as she can* mean? This is where triggers come into play (next chapter). After Julie has identified her triggers, she also understands that she will most likely need to eliminate a fifty-five and up community from her options as she is deciding to take that step in her current home. As Julie's Aging Advisor I would educate her on CCRCs (Continued Care Retirement Communities), Independent Living, and Assisted Living, because if and when her next transition occurs it will most likely be to one of those types of communities. She also has the option to use her funds to bring full services into her home so she never has to leave, but she will need to understand what it could potentially cost, and she might not have the funds to have 24-hour caregivers at home in her plan.

The goal of this pillar is designed for you to first choose the location you plan to age in, so when you are gaining education on your potential living options for the future you can decide between one or two in your area and let your support system know which ones you would be okay with. What a relief to your support system to know that when they are at a point in helping you with big decisions, they already know you have vetted and chosen what would be acceptable to you. They will also know you have thought about the finances associated with it.

In Chapter 1, we discussed having a support system and how to identify yours. Identifying your support system plays a big part in identifying your potential aging living options. For example, if you decided that your adult daughter will be your support system, but she lives in a different state, do you plan to move to that state? If the answer is no, then you need to educate yourself on a professional support system, like a care manager, who you can put into place locally to support your distant support system.

If you are okay with moving to another state, another decision must be made. Do you move when you are one-hundred-percent independent and can create a social scene for yourself (part time job, volunteer, church, etc.)? Or are you happy with your current social scene so you are waiting until "triggers" occur. Depending on the triggers you identify, it may mean that you know that when you move closer to your daughter, you are going into a community living environment. At least knowing there could potentially be a day when you move to another state will allow you to be ahead of the game, and your support system will have peace of mind that you have a plan and that the plan works for everyone.

The "Home" pillar is vitally important, as is a plan for your living environment, because I have heard so many times throughout my career… "I promised Mom, I wouldn't put her in a home." Every time I hear that phrase it makes me cringe. First, how unfair it is to make this promise to someone. We cannot predict the future, and our support system is under no obligation to put a stop to their life and disengage from their families and career to make sure we are not placed in a "home." They should also not be responsible for us continuing to live in an unsafe and unrealistic environment. Let us be thoughtful, competent, and realistic enough about what we are asking of our support system and let us realize that support from our living environment can keep us independent longer…and in control.

6

PILLAR 3 – SUPPORTIVE SERVICES

Without fail, at least once a week in any of the senior living communities I was the director of, we would get a phone call asking if we took such and such insurance. This continued to surprise me repeatedly. Most of the time it was an adult child calling because Mom was either in the hospital or completing a short-term stay in a rehabilitation center and a doctor told the family that Mom was not able to live alone anymore. This question showed how unprepared the family was in dealing with the next step of Mom's aging journey.

Can you imagine the surprise and shock when I not only told the caller that health insurance does not cover assisted living but that our apartments started at five-thousand dollars per month *before* we determined care charges and/or medication charges? The feeling of panic on the other side of the phone was evident without any further exchange of words. A crisis was a common time for the family of an aging individual to learn about the finances of their loved one. Is this really the time you want an education on your options when you are not capable of visiting potential communities and giving your feedback? You are leaving all options to your support system and then they must try to be a detective with your money and assets to see what you can even afford.

I hope this is one of the reasons you are reading this book. So, you can become an educated consumer and already have an idea of what you can afford and where you would like to go if certain things happen along your aging journey. Not only will this ensure you keep control of your aging goals and desires, but it will be such a gift to your support system, so they do not experience the panic and chaos that an unplanned aging journey brings to so many.

I define "supportive service" as any service you are provided to support your functional needs. These services are either paid for by private funds or covered by health- or long-term care insurance.

Here is a list of potential supportive services:

- ✓ Professional support system
- ✓ Home Care
- ✓ Home Health
- ✓ Home Safety Services
- ✓ Transportation Services
- ✓ Medication Management
- ✓ Cleaning Services
- ✓ Home Maintenance Services
- ✓ Meal Services
- ✓ Living Options
- ✓ Support Groups

There are a few ways I determine the services in which my clients should be educated: their medical history and any current diagnosis along with family history that can predict future needs. Decisions made in pillars 1 and 2 also guide our supportive service conversation.

For example, if my client wants to stay in their current home throughout their aging journey, they will receive a comprehensive education on the difference between home care and home health, and not only how the services work but how to best use them. Most individuals are not even aware of the smorgasbord of resources available to them, so they do not ever access them. Utilizing supportive services early and in the right way will allow you to stay independent longer.

Triggers

Let us have a conversation about Triggers.

Triggers are defined as a "cause (an event or situation) that happens or exists."

I have witnessed thousands of families experience a common theme: the lack of ability of the aging individual to identify when it is time to make a change or introduce a new service. This creates a lot of stress and heartache for the support system. They find themselves not only unprepared or ill-equipped to talk with their loved ones about the decline they are seeing, but they must also acknowledge how the decline and lack of recognition for adjustments is causing stress and resentfulness for them.

Now that I work with individual clients, this is one of the most common reasons I am asked to come in and help families. Personal support people tell me, "Mom won't accept any help, but she is not safe, and I am overwhelmed and stressed out." Identifying triggers early and throughout the aging plan allows for everyone to be on the same page, plus it gives black-and-white occurrences where additional services or a transition makes sense. For example, Ruby wants to stay home as long as she can. Her home has been determined to be safe and she is fine with bringing in any services needed to stay in her home. When evaluating Ruby's funds, she does have to be mindful not to spend more than ten-thousand dollars a month for her money to last at least five years. Home care is on average between $25-$55 an hour. A trigger Ruby had to put into place is that when services at home such as Home care start to cost more than ten thousand a month, she knows she will have to move to Assisted Living. Of course, Ruby is hoping it never happens, but at least she has chosen the Assisted Living she will move to if the scenario becomes a reality. That is how one keeps control, and it motivates people to stay healthy by accepting support to stay in their home longer.

Another common trigger is a diagnosis for either a cognitive disorder or a neurological disorder (Parkinson's, for example). When either of these diagnoses occur, they should trigger a variety of services to start right away.

When I speak to diverse groups around the country I am often asked, "*How do I educate myself on services and become an educated consumer?*" For most people there is a prime time to educate ourselves: right after retirement and before we start to need the services we have been discussing.

I tell my clients to create an aging journey email address, as you will get blasted with emails during this education phase. It is temporary and worth it. Since there is a lack of understanding of how services work, many companies create and produce events that focus on education. Large senior living communities, senior centers, and local aging non-profits will host live and online educational opportunities. I challenge my clients to get on email lists so they can see what educational opportunities are available around them and hopefully attend many of them. The senior living communities will conduct their events in person because they want you to see the amenities, and they will always offer you drinks and food. It is an opportunity to learn about services, ask questions, and maybe meet a friend or two. These educational opportunities rarely run for more than an hour. One hour of your time is worth it to be a more prepared and educated consumer. You will be on their mailing list, but you can always unsubscribe. Also, by having a secondary email address, you know when you open that account you are mentally prepared for the marketing material you will receive. Getting educated on potential supportive services allows you to create an aging plan that is realistic and thoroughly thought-out.

7

PILLAR 4—INTENTIONAL SOCIAL ENGAGEMENT

In May 2023, Dr. Vivek Murthy issued a surgeon general's advisory raising alarm about the "Devastating Impact of the Epidemic of Loneliness and Isolation in the United States[1]." I was not surprised by the study's findings and believe it has been an issue much longer than the covid epidemic which exacerbated it. I started my career in senior living as an Activity Director in a memory care community. I received my undergraduate degree in Therapeutic Recreation, so programming and leisure are something I find a lot of value in, but my experience working with aging individuals has shown me that leisure and recreation are not values of top priority. During my tenure as an activity director, I noticed that

---

1 Murthy, Vivek. "Devastating Impact of the Epidemic of Loneliness and Isolation in the United States." hhs.gov. https://www.hhs.gov/about/news/2023/05/03/new-surgeon-general-advisory-raises-alarm-about-devastating-impact-epidemic-loneliness-isolation-united-states.html. (Accessed January 9, 2024).

the first thing in a community to get compromised or cancelled was programming. It was not a priority, nor do most Executive Directors push the associates to actively participate in programming. I guess the communities that I directed were a little different as I put a lot of priority on programming and felt, at times, it was more important than some of the medical issues we had to deal with. If residents were engaged and socially fulfilled, they were healthier all around and stayed independent longer. This is a philosophy I still hold in high regard and is why intentional social engagement planning is the fourth pillar in my aging success matrix.

Let us revisit the most common request I hear: "I want to stay in my home." When one of my clients has requested to stay in their home, I absolutely add this pillar to my planning for them.

To plan successfully, the idea of self-awareness comes back into play. If you are someone who has a tough time being introspective and honest with yourself, this pillar may take a bit longer to work through.

The first conversation I have with clients when working on this pillar is to help them identify their "3 Rs."

Roles – What do they do? How someone spent their time during their working years is a big indicator of how they recreate. What occupation did they have? And if more than one, which one did they do at the peak of their happiness in their work life? Someone who chose teaching as a career is going to have a different personality than a satisfied accountant. Were they domestic leaders? And, if so, did they enjoy the role or did they feel, due to societal constraints, that was their only option?

Relationships – What relationships do you have in your life? Are you a mother, grandmother, aunt, uncle?

Do you struggle with intimate relationships, or do you have many significant long-term relationships in your life? Remember, there is no wrong answer; self-awareness will help your aging journey feel successful.

Recreation – What hobbies did you have? How do you recreate? When you join groups, do you strive to be in a leadership position or are you more of a passive participant? Do you enjoy mission/purpose-driven recreation (volunteering or task-driven), or do you feel satisfied and happy socially recreating (book clubs, card clubs, happy hour)?

Here is an example of how one of my clients managed his aging journey:

Richard was a successful business owner and worked until he was close to eighty. He loved the work he did and was exceptionally good at it. When Richard retired, he quickly declined and ended up needing assisted living fairly quickly. It is important to note that Richard should have retired years before his eightieth birthday as his son was already running his business and he was just there for posterity. This scenario is not the best way to age because Richard had put all his social engagement and purpose into his role at his company.

This is a common scenario with men. Their role consumes their identity, and they lack the insight or true knowledge of how they recreate. If Richard had been proactive about his social engagement as he aged, he may have decided to cut back his hours at his job and start volunteering in the community. There are a multitude of non-profits looking for accomplished and experienced individuals who have the time to invest on their board. Richard could have used his expertise to find a new purpose that would be more appropriate for retirement living. He would have stayed healthy and independent longer because his transition would have made sense for how he recreated.

Women are more likely to be social recreators which results in being able to find easier access to activities as we age. Intentional social engagement is determined by figuring out if you are a purposeful recreator or a social recreator.

When discussing social engagement, the next area I dive into with my clients is how they receive their energy. This is extroversion vs. introversion. When you are an extrovert, you draw energy from being around others. Introversion is the opposite. You may like being around others, but when it comes to recharging, your body wants to do that alone or in a very intimate setting. As we age and our social world gets smaller and we add future potential issues that may prevent us from independently recreating, we need to be proactive on how to continue to fulfill our needs. The recommendations I give my clients are determined by whether they are extroverted or introverted.

Ed is an eighty-four-year-old man who is living in the house he has lived in for forty years. His wife has been very resistant to changing the environment even though the house is in general disrepair and their social life has gotten significantly smaller. Ed is the epitome of an extrovert. You could say Ed never met a stranger, and the more social events he has the better he feels. Ed receives his energy from others. In all honesty, so does his wife, but she is having a harder time with aging and is very resistant. Thirteen years ago, Ed wanted to move into a fifty-five and up community, but he could not convince his wife.

Now thirteen years later Ed has a challenging time holding conversations and spends his day sitting on the couch watching TV. He was recently diagnosed with cognitive decline. I am not a doctor, but I feel strongly that if Ed had been able to live in an environment for the last five to eight years where all he had to do was go out of his condo and be surrounded by others, or if he had a social event like happy hour to attend, Ed's cognitive health would now be in a much better place.

By spending the last five years disengaged from others and only social when people came to him, his need for energy from others was not being met. This is not good for Ed's cognition or any other extrovert who is aging.

Extroverts

Let us start with my extroverted clients. These clients need social interaction to recharge, and it is good for their brain health. When it comes to this specific group of clients, we start educating them on community living.

Introverts

For clients who are naturally introverted, we discuss the idea of how to organize accessing social events as they age. Even if you are an introvert, being around others at least a little bit of time is important, but you would have to be a little more strategic since community living is going to sound like the worst idea.

Education for introverts centers around locating companion services and finding out how to best use them. We may discuss how to use your support system to access the small amount of social engagement you need. We talk about the idea that as you age, as an introvert you will want to use supportive services to help you continue the social activities that you do enjoy yet, at the same time, be in a place where you can recharge. Introverted clients are the ones most likely to want to stay in their home, but I must remind them that if they need care, they are going to have someone in their private home many hours per day. Are they going to feel like they must talk with their caregiver? Are they going to get annoyed that the care provider is just sitting on the couch in between their scheduled tasks?

If the idea of someone in your home several hours a day sounds bad, we would talk about community living where you would have your own private space, and care only comes to you when you need it. For some introverts this makes sense.

The goal of the conversation is for you as the individual to take a hard look at who you are, how you recreate, how you rejuvenate and how you receive energy. You would then reach out to us to help you make future decisions that make the most sense for you. It will allow you to enter the decision educated and prepared for what is to come.

Intergenerational Therapy

Many of my clients talk about living around younger people. This desire or wish is a common pushback for someone who is trying to find any reason to stay in the home where they currently live. There is a therapeutic phrase for living and recreating with younger people. It is called *Intergenerational Therapy*. You may recall at the beginning of this book that I am by education a Recreational Therapist, and I took an entire course on intergenerational therapy and its importance. I do believe that, as we age, the need to be strategic and thoughtful when it comes to being around younger people is important; however, your neighborhood is *not* the place to get it unless you have chosen a co-housing community where one of the missions, philosophy, and expectations of living there is to take care of all neighbors young and old. Most neighborhoods nowadays are filled with busy families shuffling children to and from activities.

There are ways to acquire intergenerational energy which I do believe can help with vitality and youthfulness. Volunteering at the local elementary school, getting a part-time job, and, of course, making a point to establish and nurture a relationship with the young family members in your life: grandchildren, and nieces and nephews.

Living around your young neighbors is not a reason to stay in a living situation that does not make sense and will not serve you well in the future. An Aging Advisor can help you look at your local community and, based on your 3 Rs, can help you recognize and create opportunities for intergenerational social engagement.

Grandma Helen

My grandmother Helen was one of the most independent women I have ever met. She was fierce and not afraid to live life to the fullest. She was also one of the people who would never even think of moving to a senior community because she did not want to "be around old people," even though she herself was over eighty years old.

As her granddaughter, who just so happened to work with seniors, I had a lot of *big* conversations with my grandmother about senior living. At that time, you could say I had drunk the Kool-Aid and thought senior living was a great option for EVERYONE. We enjoyed wine and shrimp cocktails as I expressed my fears about her living in a transient apartment complex. She would remind me that she felt one-hundred-percent safe. She would ask me a lot of questions about senior living so there were times I thought I had her convinced...but she NEVER had any intention of moving.

Let us also note that she was one-hundred-percent independent and had no medical issues that I could predict would cause her issues in the future, so she was safe and appropriate to live in her apartment. What my grandma Helen showed me was that aging *is* under our control and we can be successful at it if we make smart choices and keep ourselves engaged. My grandma got herself a part-time job at Kohl's when she was eighty-five and worked there until age ninety. She never wanted people to consider her as *old*, so even when Kohl's scheduled her for the 7pm-10pm shift she would never complain and would simply do her job.

If you have not guessed, my grandmother was not a social recreator, she was a purposeful recreator. She did not need the money, but she liked having a job, and having responsibility for something was her way of finding fulfillment. She loved being around the younger associates even though they drove her crazy with, in her opinion, their lack of job etiquette and work ethic. Kohl's job kept her sharp and was something she found pride in when she was able to tell someone she was still working. I swear this is what kept her not only young but happy as she aged.

Unfortunately, Grandma Helen was diagnosed with cancer in October of her ninety-first year and passed away in January. She chose not to go through any treatment. She passed peacefully with family around her in the apartment she had loved and stubbornly proved to everyone was the right fit for her. Grandma Helen was a fighter! She always found the good in any situation and chose to live a life where she was always doing what she wanted to do.

Choose Wisely

The worst thing we can do for ourselves is to live in a place that does not make sense and then stay there and not have our social engagement needs met, which makes for a lonely journey. It also puts a lot of pressure on your support system. You cannot rely on your adult children or family members to fulfill your entire social existence for you. Most likely your support system has a career they have worked hard at and may be at the top of their game and could also be raising children. It is *your* responsibility to be intentional and thoughtful of your social engagement.

If you are fine with living a quiet life with not many social obligations, go for it, but just be prepared that your length of life may be shortened. You may not realize how loneliness can affect your quality of life. Personalized and appropriate social engagement keeps us healthy and independent longer. If you do not fulfill that need, you must expect a shorter life and more health issues along the way. Remember, at the beginning of this book I said there is no right or wrong answer...well, here is one of those decisions you will have to consider that will drastically affect your aging journey.

If you are fully aware of the positive and negative consequences of your decision, then the choice is yours. I duly warn you that if you place your pride of staying in your home no matter what and your social engagement second, your health will suffer. I have seen it happen too many times.

8

INTERLOCKING PILLARS

I am sure you noticed while reading this book that the pillars can overlap, and how each person moves through the pillars is unique to their specific situation. Every decision you make affects the options and subsequent questions you may have regarding the other pillars. Everyone needs to start with the identification of their support system and then you can move within the pillars as it makes sense.

If you determine staying home is what you want to do, then you will quickly move out of Pillar 2 "Home" and dive deep into Pillar 3—Supportive Services. I cannot reiterate enough that throughout this process there are no right or wrong answers.

Next, I am going to give a few examples of how the pillars can be used in real case studies.

Carol and Fred

Carol and Fred retired to North Carolina fifteen years ago from Connecticut. They chose NC because of the weather and the medical systems. They have two daughters, and when they moved to NC both daughters were in the process of getting advanced degrees and had not yet settled into life. Fifteen years later both their daughters are technically settled and married with children. One daughter lives in Ohio and the other in Kentucky.

Carol and Fred have a great social circle in NC and are still regularly active in the community, and Carol is involved with several social clubs. They live in a patio home in which they could easily age. Even though Carol and Fred are still active and healthy they know they must decide how best to navigate their aging if either of them starts having health issues. Carol and Fred first need to talk about which one of their daughters they would feel the most comfortable living nearby. If they look at both daughters equally and both are in a life position to support, then they would need to research which state has the best benefits for aging.

If money is a concern for the future, they need to research which state has the best support and least amount of taxes. Every decision must be considered as a fact-finding mission. Yes, I understand that moving to Kentucky or Ohio was probably never in Carol and Fred's plan, but if being close to their children if they need support is a goal then they will have to embrace and thrive in a state they may never have thought they would live. Carol and Fred have done the research, and based on their likes, dislikes, and financial situation, moving to Kentucky will make the most sense if they ever need support.

Keep in mind, this is not a plan that is going to happen; this is simply thinking through potential decisions before you must make them in a crisis. Kentucky has been identified, so the next decision or thought process then moves to when. Do they move when they are one-hundred-percent independent and can create a life for themselves on their terms in Kentucky? Or do they wait until they need support and at that point they may move into a senior living or independent living community? If waiting until they need support is the decision, then every time they visit their daughter they should be researching and visiting potential living situations and social opportunities and getting to know the area.

As Carol and Fred's Aging Advisor, together we also identify triggers that make sense for them and their daughter so no one can argue about when the transition needs to happen. The triggers could be something as small as more than two doctor's visits a month, a specific diagnosis, or a large and life-changing event like when they no longer feel comfortable driving or have their doctor has told them that one of them should not drive anymore. The wonderful thing about this plan is that when Carol and Fred determine it is time to move, they know exactly where they will go and which option they can afford.

Joe

Joe lives in an apartment in Alabama. He is divorced and has never remarried. He has three children but only talks to one of them and she lives in Florida. He feels comfortable having her as Power of Attorney but has no intention of ever moving to Florida. His health is starting to decline, but he has a good social network where he lives. As Joe's Aging Advisor I would recommend to Joe and his daughter that he needs to budget and hire a Care Manager. He may only need to meet with his Care Manager every three to six months but establishing that relationship is key. Joe also needs to start educating himself on community living and why moving into a community would be a good option since he does not have a local personal support system. As he ages it will become expensive to rely on a professional support system like a Care Manager as his only local support. It makes more financial sense to move to a community where a support system is built in, then he only uses his Care Manager for areas that the community does not support. Joe and his daughter can put triggers in place where they both feel comfortable if the decision comes for Joe to move to Florida. In Joe's situation it would be based on finances and if his care becomes expensive, which is hard to predict.

Debra

Debra lives in Durham, North Carolina and all four of her children live in the area. Debra has also grown up in the area, so generations of relatives live in the area. Debra feels comfortable with all her children being her support system. As her Aging Advisor we identify specific roles each child can take. For example, Debra wants her two daughters to be the primary healthcare proxies (go to doctor's appointments), but she would like her one son to oversee her bills if she ever needs that support. Her youngest son will be helpful with ensuring Debra's errands are taken care of like ordering food, medicine, and any home maintenance that needs attention. We also have a family conversation to ensure everyone feels comfortable with their roles and we help identify any fears or concerns as they watch their mom get older. Debra is still very independent, and her home makes sense to live in for now. Identifying her support system and specific goals allows her family to know the expectations and to also avoid any conflict as Debra does age.

Creating an Aging Plan does *not* mean that decisions are set in stone. Aging is unpredictable and sometimes we must adjust our plans for the unexpected. What having the plan does is allow for you to already have educated yourself so if you must shift your plan, you are not starting from scratch. You have a big picture goal, and you can adjust your plan to hopefully evolve with your situation while keeping your overall goal intact.

CONCLUSION

You made it! You have done what so many have avoided. By finishing this book, you are already going to have more control of your aging journey.

As we conclude this conversation and you have acknowledged the elephant in the room, I want to talk about the common themes expressed in this book.

We are all getting older—that is a fact! Even though aging is a universal issue, our personal situation is one-hundred-percent unique. After working through your own pillars, my hope is that you have conversations with your friends about *their* pillars, which would lead to remarkably interesting conversations. You will find yourself shocked that, even though the format for an aging plan is universal, each person's aging plan is so diverse. Make it a game!

Planning for the future and getting an education on the potential choices you may have to make during your aging journey is an insurance plan. I hope you do not have to utilize some of the planning you have prepared for.

I believe that by being knowledgeable consumers and having an idea of the choices you may encounter while aging will help you stay independent and in control longer. Completing the pillars will allow you to ease stress that will help you stay healthy longer.

We all need to be part of a larger conversation regarding aging. We should be able to talk about our aging journey openly and without shame. Be proud of all you have accomplished, but also acknowledge that there may come a time where you will need a little support. By staying self-aware of who we are and identifying our aging goals and desires we can dismiss the idea that older people are dependent and weaker. Let us change the conversation and keep control while we age.

Do not let finances be the reason you do not plan for your aging journey. Your aging plan should be based on your finances. To do this successfully, an aging plan needs to be developed at least five to seven years before you may need to utilize it.

For some of you this journey might have been emotional, and it brought up personal issues that were not easy to work through. Congratulate yourself on walking through the journey anyway! You have taken a step that will ensure you will have a more successful aging journey…give yourself a high-five.

If you need support in facilitating your aging plan, please go to www.openlyaging.com/book

During our journey through this book, I have equipped you to create a successful aging plan, and I look forward to hearing the stories from those who are ready to take control.

Finally, as we finish, I would like you to acknowledge the gift and legacy you are giving to your loved ones—all your loved ones, not just your identified support system. As your loved ones watch you take a proactive approach to aging, everyone involved will experience less stress, and taking initiative for your aging journey will also allow relationships to thrive and those around you to extend support naturally and with ease.

By *Openly Aging*, you are leaving a legacy of control and independence that will be carried on for generations.

About the Author

Allison O'Shea is a leader in the aging industry. She has over twenty years of direct hands-on experience working with seniors and their families in the role of Executive Director for various senior living companies. This experience has given her the knowledge to be a reputable voice in the confusing and overwhelming world of aging.

In January of 2022 Allison founded Openly Aging, LLC and created the profession of Aging Advisor. An Aging Advisor is a professional who works with an aging person and their family to gather the information needed to create a long- and short-term strategy to maintain independence as long as possible while being educated on all their options for the future. The Aging Advisor along with the client and family then determine which path is best based on key elements, support system, finances, current living situation and future options and intentional social engagement.

Everyone's aging path is different. Allison and her clients engage in open dialogue about what is important to them, and then create a strategy of education so her clients maintain independence and control throughout their aging journey.

The mission of Openly Aging is to talk about the elephant in the room...aging...and be thoughtful about how we embark on our aging journey.

Acknowledgements

I had no idea the journey I would embark on when I decided to start Openly Aging after twenty years in the corporate world. There have been times of very big highs and times of very low lows but there has never been a time where I regretted making such a drastic career move.

I could not have written this book without the help and support of Michelle Hill and the Winning Proof team—your expertise and guidance through this process have been invaluable and I truly could not have written and published this book without you.

I mentioned my parents, Dennis and Maryellen, a few times in the book as they have been my biggest supporters, not only in the creation of Openly Aging, but throughout my life. They have also been my muses while writing this book as they are doing retirement correctly, living their best life while being open about their aging journeys.

Twenty-two years ago, when I met a cute golfer at Belmont Abbey College, I had no idea that boy would turn into the man I owe everything to. Seventeen years of marriage and two amazing children later, I would have never dreamed of where my life would be. The days I wanted to give up Chris was right there encouraging me to continue. He believed in my vision and trusted my career choices even when I questioned them myself. Thank you to Chris and our beautiful children, Jack and Emily.

CONNECT WITH ALLISON

Allison would love to speak at your company, upcoming conference, retreat, meeting, or as a guest on your podcast.

To book, email Allison at allison.oshea@openlyaging.com

Let's connect on social media:
https://www.facebook.com/openlyaging
https://www.instagram.com/openlyaging/
https://www.linkedin.com/in/allison-o-shea/
If you are a fan of this book, please tell others…

- ➢ Write about *Openly Aging* on your blog and social media channels.

- ➢ Feature Allison on your podcast or radio/TV broadcast.

- ➢ Suggest this book to your friends, family, neighbors, and coworkers.

- ➢ Write an authentic, positive review on Amazon. com.

- ➢ Take a selfie of you holding the book, then post and tag Allison on your social media channels.

- ➢ Purchase additional copies for the openly aging people in your life or to give away as gifts.

www.ingramcontent.com/pod-product-compliance
Lightning Source LLC
Chambersburg PA
CBHW051234120626
46547CB00013B/1638